Enfield Libraries

Please remember that this item will attract overdue charges
if not returned by the latest date stamped above. You may
renew it in person, by telephone or by post quoting the
barcode number and your library card number.

ENFIELD
Leisure Services
working for people

THE ASSOCIATION FOR INFORMATION MANAGEMENT

imi   INFORMATION MANAGEMENT INTERNATIONAL

30126 01451381 3

Published by Aslib, The Association for Information Management and Information Management International
Staple Hall
Stone House Court
London EC3A 7PB
Tel: +44 20 7 903 0000
Fax: +44 20 7 903 0011
Email: *aslib@aslib.co.uk*
WWW: *http://www.aslib.co.uk/*

ISBN 0 85142 424 4

How to Promote Your Web Site Effectively

Mark Kerr

THE ASSOCIATION FOR INFORMATION MANAGEMENT

INFORMATION MANAGEMENT INTERNATIONAL

Is your organisation a corporate member of Aslib?

Aslib, The Association for Information Management is a world class corporate membership organisation with over 2000 members in some 70 countries. Aslib actively promotes best practice in the management of information resources. It lobbies on all aspects of the management of, and legislation concerning, information at local, national and international levels.

Aslib provides consultancy and information services, professional development training, conferences, specialist recruitment, Internet products, and publishes primary and secondary journals, conference proceedings, directories and monographs.

Further information is available from:

Aslib, The Association for Information Management
Staple Hall
Stone House Court
London EC3A 7PB
Tel: +44 20 7 903 0000
Fax: +44 20 7 903 0011
Email: *aslib@aslib.co.uk*
WWW: *http://www.aslib.co.uk/*

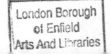

Series Editor

Sylvia Webb is a well known consultant, author and lecturer in the information management field. Her first book, *Creating an Information Service*, now in its third edition, was published by Aslib and has sold in over forty countries. She has experience of working in both the public and private sectors, ranging from public libraries to national and international organisations. She has also been a lecturer at Ashridge Management College, specialising in management and interpersonal skills, which led to her second book, *Personal Development in Information Work*, also published by Aslib. She has served on a number of government advisory bodies and is past Chair of the Information and Library Services Lead Body which develops National Vocational Qualifications (NVQs) for the LIS profession. She is actively involved in professional education with Aslib and the Library Association and is also a former Vice-President of the Institute of Information Scientists. As well as being editor of this series, Sylvia Webb has written three of the Know How Guides: *Making a charge for library and information services*, *Preparing a guide to your library and information service* and *Knowledge management: linchpin of change*.

A complete listing of all titles in the series can be found at the back of this volume.

About the author

Mark Kerr is Centre Manager at London Aspect, a Business Link advice and local support centre based at South Bank University. In this role he provides advice, training and support to companies and organisations seeking to benefit from their activities on the Internet. Previously he was Internet Training Coordinator, developing – and delivering – a range of public courses in Web publishing, Internet marketing and research, and business use of the Internet.

Mark has also written *Web Publishing: An Introduction to HTML*, published by LITC in 1998. He is CD-ROM Reviews Editor for *Library Technology* magazine, and has contributed articles to *VINE*, *Library Technology* and *Multimedia Information and Technology*, as well as contributing book reviews to a number of publications, including *Managing Information*.

Contents

Introduction

Web sites are increasingly a central part of the library or information service. Whilst some may have once been limited to a simple listing of services and contacts, Web sites now contain primary information, bibliographic resources, helpsheets, feedback and enquiry forms, access to other online services, registration and subscription services, searchable catalogues, Web-delivered training and more.

Whether your Web site contains all or any of these services, some effort has gone into the design and development of the site. If no one knows about it, then that effort is wasted. This book is intended to ensure that your efforts are not only recognised, but rewarded – by ensuring that your client group is aware of the services available on your Web site, and by further ensuring that this same client group expands.

Throughout this book, the phrase 'information service' should be taken to include libraries, marketing departments, in fact all areas of 'information' activities within an organisation whether public or private sector, commercial or non-profit, academic or research, free or priced, loan or reference. The mission of all these types of information service is essentially the same – to enable access to relevant information, in a timely, appropriate and cost-effective manner.

Although written primarily for information services that wish to develop and promote their Web sites, the techniques in this book can be applied equally to entertainment, commercial or personal Web sites. Most Web activities have something in common – a desire to communicate, some content to deliver. This book seeks to ensure that whatever the nature of the site, its content can be presented to the widest possible audience.

Note

To aid illustration and examples in this book, I have used the entirely fictitious *AskAtTheDesk Information Ltd.* Any resemblance to any organisation is entirely unintentional. A name search on the Equifax database, through InterNic and on the Web revealed no pre-existing organisations using this name. All other examples and illustrations in this book are used as demonstrations of good practice or effective services, for purposes of review and are to the benefit of the trademark owner.

The more practical parts of this book include some HTML code. Although knowledge of HTML is not required to use most of the advice contained here, some understanding of HTML will help in the implementation of the design features in Chapter 3 and Chapter 5.

1. Why Promote?

A decision to design and develop a Web site is usually based on a range of factors – widening access to information, improving communication with a number of audiences, dissemination of research results, cost-savings over traditional delivery methods, improving the organisation's efficiency. Occasionally, the motivating factor may simply be that 'everyone else has one'.

The benefits of an effective information-based Web site can be several and significant, falling into one of three areas:

- resource justification;
- fulfilling the mission;
- cost savings.

Investment of time and resources can be justified by high usage of the resulting resource. The profile of the library or information service can be raised, ensuring a greater recognition for the role within the organisation, with a possible positive impact on future funding decisions.

The information service's mission – whether stated or implicit – to provide easy access to relevant and timely information can be enhanced by providing Web-based information. Direct access to a database, or simply organisational information (opening hours, location, contact details, and frequently asked questions) all support the delivery of the service.

Transferring some printed resources online can reduce costs. Revenues may be increased if subscriptions or sales are promoted, or even directly
available, online. Staff time can be saved – or used
more effectively – if 'standard' questions can be pre-
dicted and answered through an online FAQ (Frequently Asked Questions) service. Access can be
provided to users beyond your immediate location,
and beyond your typical opening hours.

These benefits apply to virtually all libraries and
information services. Some will have the resources,
time and inclination to exploit them fully – and will
have already done so – whilst others will only be
able to develop online services gradually as resources become available.

Whilst these benefits support the case for a Web
site, building the resource is just the first step. Marketing your online information service is as important – if not more so – as 'real world' marketing
activities. No matter how familiar your users may
be with your service, new resources need to be promoted. If you are actively seeking new users – or
aiming for greater use by the existing user base –
then effective promotion is not just desirable, it is
essential.

Audiences

Whatever the range of information or services
within the Web site, and whatever the nature of
your information service, it is likely that you will
have more than one target audience.

Core and non-core

Academic libraries serve several audiences: students, teaching staff and researchers are the core group, each with different needs. But external users from different institutions, sectors or countries may also use the services. The quality of the Web site may have a bearing on recruitment or on funding opportunities, for example.

Internal and External

Commercial, corporate and special libraries' Web sites may be targeted at a known and limited audience (which may of course be enormous) – particularly if the Web site is restricted to intranet access. But even here there are multiple definable user groups with different requirements. Marketing, production and research may all need information, but at different times and in different formats. Where the information service has a role – implied or explicit – as part of the wider marketing and PR activities of an organisation, this audience may include suppliers, clients, interested professionals, competitors and students, regulatory bodies or the general public.

New or Existing

As an existing service, you will have some knowledge of your current audience or market. However, they may be unaware of your new online services. Internal marketing and promotion can often be more important – and more easily overlooked – than external or public marketing activities.

Your Web site design and content will take into account your core audience, whilst ensuring that non-core visitors will also be able to derive some benefit from their exploration of your site. There may be restricted areas requiring passwords, but there will also be some public information – at the very least, information about the service and details on who may access it, and how.

One of the key strengths of the Web is its ability to target niche markets effectively. Whatever the special focus or coverage of your information service, there are likely to be potential visitors who are entirely unaware of your existence. They may be the other side of the world, or simply working in a sector not obviously related to yours.

Using the techniques outlined in this book, you have an opportunity to reach both your existing audience, and also that audience about whom you know little or nothing. There is a wide range of strategies to ensure maximum exposure for your information service. Not every activity will apply to every organisation, but selection of the most relevant activities will maximise your chances of being visible in the confused environment of the World Wide Web.

For the purposes of this book, I have made a few assumptions:

- you seek to maximise use of your Web site;
- the information provided is non-confidential;
- the information is 'safe' for public use.

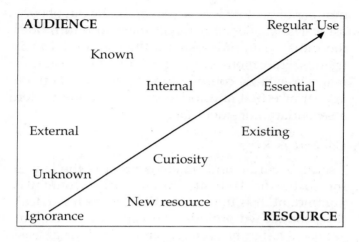

Diagram 1: the further up the diagonal arrow, the less effort required to promote the resource

If your particular service does not meet these assumptions, then simply pick and choose those activities that are appropriate. Private information should be protected by password or intranet – simply keeping quiet about a globally visible Web page is not a valid security strategy! You should of course also ensure that appropriate disclaimers are highly visible, particularly where legal or health information is concerned.

Clichés and Truisms

If you build it, they will come

This quotation from the Kevin Costner film *Field of Dreams* has become a cliché in Web design advice. It's even true, up to a point. You can expect a number of visitors who access your site out of curiosity. The challenge is to get them to return after the initial visit, to bookmark the site, to tell their friends. Enormous effort goes into the design of many Web sites, concentrating all too often on the appearance first and foremost, with content often a secondary consideration.

Content is King

Useful, accurate and timely content is the key to the successful Web site. In our sector, content is paramount. It is the commodity in which we deal, the product we provide, the very reason for our service. Design has often been ignored, or at least overlooked in favour of the content. Clearly the best sites combine both content and design in a complementary manner – information is more accessible through good design. But if no one knows about the resource, the effort is wasted. The effective Web site combines and balances the three key features – design, content and promotion.

Size Matters

Building the Web's biggest resource in your subject area is not synonymous with building the Web's best resource. The content of the World Wide Web is expanding at around 1-1.5 million pages per day. What your users need is access to the relevant information for their interests, preferably sorted, assessed, described by someone they trust. Of course they also want to browse for the unexpected materials – your Web site will be just one of their information sources: but it should be their favourite one.

The Alta Vista index contains over 130,000,000 pages. Yahoo!'s directory contains over 700,000 sites. EEVL has 'only' 3,400 sites in its catalogue, OMNI 3,500, RUDI 1,500, Biz/ED 1,100 – but they are all evaluated and described, all relevant to their particular subject area. Most of these sites might be findable in Yahoo! or Alta Vista, but only with an extraordinary expenditure of time and effort. Smaller, focused resources can be far more effective for specific needs than the Web giants.

The Faster the Better

Accessing the required information on a Web site should be easy and fast. Attractive and effective navigational and information design should enable the user to find the information they are after with the minimum of backtracking or unnecessary browsing. Graphics should be optimised for fast downloading, and the overall use of graphics should reflect an awareness of the users' technology. If your typical user is on JANET, the UK universities' network, it may be acceptable to use extensive graphics. If, however, your site is designed for global access, particularly from countries with slower connections, then a different design approach may be appropriate. The table below shows one view of the proportion of Web users with different speeds of connection:

Modem speed	% of users
Less than 14.4k	0.1%
14.4k	1.7%
28.8k	15.4%
33.6k	17.7%
56k	31.4%
ISDN or faster	6.0%

*Source: GTRC, GVU's 10th WWW User Survey October 1998
at: http://www.gvu.gatech.edu/user_surveys*

This shows over 65% of users have a connection speed slower than that of ISDN. Your design therefore should take account of this, depending on the proportion of your users that you *know* to be on faster network connections.

2. Promotional Strategy

A marketing and promotion strategy is composed of a number of elements: internal improvements to the service itself (in this case to the Web site), specific promotional campaigns, recognition of the importance of commitment from both customer and provider. Setting the strategy is not a once-only event; it is part of a continuous process. The process illustrated below is not set in concrete – choose those elements that apply to your service, adapt them to your specific circumstance, and build them into your operational planning.

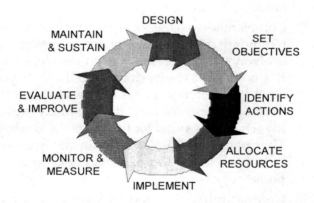

Diagram 2. The Promotional Strategy Cycle

Design

Promoting a Web site is about more than attracting new visitors: it includes ensuring that an initial visit becomes a regular event. This is done largely by ensuring that the content and design of the site is such that it becomes an essential part of the information resource collection of the desired visitor. Although this book is not intended to be a guide to site design, there are some aspects of creating and developing a Web site that contribute greatly to its usability, and consequently its success:

- Accuracy – links lead where they claim to lead, text spellchecked, content proof-read.

- Topicality – *'last updated'* or *'page created'* dates clear (and recent!), out of date material deleted, or moved to archive area.

- Accessibility – content clearly distinguished from illustrative and navigational images and links.

- Completeness – *'Under construction'* notices are redundant. By definition, every good Web site is always under review and in development. If a page isn't ready, don't publish it. If you must have 'empty' pages as placeholders for imminent new content, then explain explicitly what is intended for that page – and when. That page should also contain navigational links back to the top of the section, or to the home page.

- Compatibility – tested in various popular browsers, on a Mac and a PC, and with images turned off: if it still makes sense *and* looks good, then the site has been well designed.

Set Objectives

These may be very general, and possibly difficult to measure:

- supporting your central mission;
- raising the Web site or information service's profile;
- improving access to your information resources.

They may be very specific and quantifiable:

- achieving a certain number of daily or weekly site 'hits';
- generating enquiries, bookings, membership subscriptions;
- revenue targets for priced services;
- a *reduction* in telephone enquiries.

A timetable is also necessary. However, site promotion is not an overnight activity. For example, the time lag between submitting a site's URL to a search engine and being found from a search can be several days, and often weeks (see Chapter 6). Correcting and repeating a submission can take as long again. A realistic timetable should be developed, and flexibility built in.

Identify and Select Actions

Select from your toolkit of actions as detailed in the following six chapters, decide which will achieve specific targets, and which will contribute to overall improvements. Some may be deferred for a 'second wave' of promotion, or omitted altogether as appropriate. The core actions are:

- designing for searchability;
- URL submission;
- establishing links;
- inclusive and internal promotion;
- press releases and online announcements;
- direct advertising.

Allocate Resources and Distribute Responsibilities

Although all promotional activities should certainly be co-ordinated, there are several benefits from breaking them down to groups of tasks that can be shared among a team. The pressure of work is reduced; ownership of the site and its activities is shared and improved – all too often the Web site is seen as an external 'add-on' that is someone else's responsibility; promotion through varying media can be conducted simultaneously, online, in print and via other communication channels; promotion can be prepared concurrently with design, saving time and sustaining team enthusiasm.

Implement

As the advert for Nike sports shoes says, *Just do it*. Once the schedule has been set, then delivering on time – and ensuring everyone who is involved does likewise – helps establish the importance of the activity within the wider information service.

Monitor and Measure

Chapter 9 describes some of the tools and techniques used to provide statistical evidence for the success of your promotional activities. Some level of measurement is essential if you are to assess the effectiveness of your strategy, and by measuring over time you can spot trends and identify opportunities for further action and improvement.

Evaluate and Improve

Continuous improvement is as important to Web site activities as to any others. It is often easier to apply, as Web site redesign and improvements can be conducted more quickly and more cheaply than in print or CD-ROM-based media. Indeed Web sites often benefit from a sense of organic growth and change, where improvements, however modest, are made frequently – the site looks 'live' and dynamic, rather than static and lifeless.

Maintain and Sustain

This applies to the Web site itself as mentioned above. But it also applies to the promotional activities. The Web is a dynamic and competitive environment. Your site is competing with other sites for the time, attention and loyalty of visitors – and for their money as well in the case of priced services. Revisiting the promotional activities, perhaps every two or three months, can ensure that you keep your audience aware and alert.

Chapters 3-8 provide a range of techniques and skills for promoting your Web site. Although you could select from these and apply them at random, designing, developing and following a clear strategy will ensure that resources and time are not wasted or duplicated.

The Promotional Toolkit

There are seven key areas of promotional activity, which combine to create an effective promotional toolkit:

- promotional strategy;
- site design;
- URL submission;
- establishing links;
- inclusive promotion;
- press releases;
- direct advertising.

The section on design is substantially larger than the others. This may seem curious in a book that is not specifically a design guide, but design is a crucial feature in the success of your promotional activities. In 'real world' marketing, it is as important to get the product and organisational style right as it is to place your advertisement in the correct magazine. Web site promotion is the same. Effective design provides its own promotional benefits. The other five key activities build on that foundation, and in combination they create an effective, practical and affordable promotional strategy.

3. Promotion by Design

There is a good deal of discussion in Internet marketing forums about the importance of search engines for site promotion. On the one hand it may seem perfectly obvious that if your site cannot be found by a search on one of the leading search services, then you may be missing large numbers of potential visitors. On the other hand, the visitors that you do get from this route may not really be the high-value committed visitors that you are really looking for. As with most debates, the true answer lies somewhere in the middle: certainly it is important to be featured in the main search services, but they may – perhaps even should – only provide a limited proportion of your visitors. As such, the time and effort devoted to a prominent presence must be proportionate to the expected results.

For a brand new service providing solutions to an existing need, search engines are a vital source of site traffic. Until and unless your site becomes well-known in your sector, there will be few links to your site from other relevant organisations' Web sites. In the early stages at least, the majority of traffic may well be from Web users conducting a search for your area of information. It is important to note that the key phrase here is *area of information* rather than your specific organisation. If they know your name and range of services, then they probably know how to contact you direct. This chapter focuses on those who need the answers, and don't yet know where to search for them – the key assumption is that you want your site to be that source of answers.

The Searching Process

To make the search engines work as a promotional tool for your site, you need to have a little understanding of how they work. This gives you the knowledge to influence the performance and position of your site in the results of a search.

Typically the non-professional searcher will go to one or two familiar search services, and put in a single keyword. When the inevitable happens – millions of unrelated hits, mostly from American sites – further action may include adding another word or two, perhaps selecting the phrase option. An informational professional may well take a different approach, perhaps using the advanced features of the same search services, perhaps constructing a Boolean search statement to enhance the accuracy and relevance of the results retrieved, and reduce their number to a manageable size. Whichever of these approaches is taken, some things are the same: both searches are conducted in the same database; all the searching software is doing – all it can do – is match strings of characters in the search term against strings of characters in the database; the results are returned to your screen in a limited format, with the supposedly relevant records at the top of the list. Even the sophisticated natural language options provided by Alta Vista and InfoSeek, where you can type in a question in plain English, end up with the search being a process of matching strings of characters. The only difference with these is that the search software translates your question into a series of search terms, with varying degrees of accuracy or success.

One other key difference between Internet searching and traditional online searching is that the Internet is a 'stateless environment'. Whereas in an online search you might carry out several preliminary searches, and then combine the results from those into a further search, on the Internet there is no 'memory' of previous searches. Each search is a brand new event for the search engine. Some services offer refined options based on previous results, but these are then combined with the original search terms and re-presented as another 'new' search.

What this all means for the Web site designer is that a good deal of thought has to go into making your site 'jump' out of the database as the result for searches, and – equally important – jump to the highest in the list of results. This chapter focuses on that task.

Searchability

To maximise the effectiveness of your page, you need to design in 'retrievability' or relevance, in other words 'searchability'. As far as the user is concerned, if your site does not appear as the result of their search then it might as well not exist. Unfortunately the nature and size of the Web means that this applies if you do not feature in the top 50-100 results. Few searchers will be likely to plough through several thousand results, and even if they do, there is little enough in the record of a search to differentiate your site. A high ranking is the only reliable way to achieve visibility in the search results, and that requires some effort and not a little ingenuity.

Understanding how search engines operate can be illuminating – and reassuring. When a user conducts a search in Alta Vista or one of the other indexing search services, the result is entirely dependent on the keywords or phrases used. A search for **steel girder** retrieves 861,070 results. A search for **+steel +girder** and then for **"steel girder"** will give very different numbers, but in each case Alta Vista will

Search terms	Boolean equivalent or comment	Number of results
steel girder	steel OR girder	861,070
+steel +girder	steel AND girder	20,360
"steel girder"	steel ADJ girder (i.e. as a phrase)	804
"steel girder" host:uk	phrase, only sites ending in .uk	26
rsj	lower or upper case	4259
RSJ	upper case only	3245
RSJ host:uk	upper case, only UK domains	142
+rsj +steel	both rsj and steel in each record	137
+rsj +steel host:uk	as above, but only in UK domains	21

attempt to rank the results so that the most relevant ones are at the top of the list.

This demonstrates both the strength and weakness of the search engines – they are large and powerful databases, but they can only respond to the information provided by the searcher. For example if you manage a Web site for a steel fabrications information service, and you typically refer to your product as "RSJs" (rolled or rigid steel joists), then your site may simply not appear as a result of the searches shown in the table above, despite the obvious (to you at least) relevance of your service to the needs of the searcher.

Getting to the Top

The indexes do not return hits at random, however it may seem at times. They compare the indexed contents of a page with the search terms entered by the user: the better the match, the higher the position. The Web page designer can affect this position by careful design. Keywords – the words you hope will match the terms used by the searcher – may appear anywhere on the page, but their position on the page will affect the score applied by the search engine when ranking the results in order of relevance.

Not all search engines index page contents in the same way. Some, like Alta Vista or HotBot, index the entire page contents. Others, like InfoSeek or Lycos, index only part of the page – perhaps the first 50 or 100 words. Most of the indexes give added weight to words in the specific parts of the page.

Keyword Selection

Choose relevant keywords carefully and use them consistently – this should not just be your brand or organisation's name, but the word – any word – a visitor might enter when searching for your activity, product or service. For example, if I wish to promote AskAtTheDesk's information services, there is little benefit to be gained from repeating the company name wherever possible. Searchers are unlikely to use that as a search term. However, as I would wish this Web site to feature in the results lists for searches for 'information providers', 'online searchers', 'research services' and 'knowledge management', these are the terms I should introduce to the page.

Identifying keywords can be as much art as science – you need to place yourself in the position of someone undertaking a Web search for which you wish to be the result. Then identify – or guess – the terms they might use in their search. Those are your primary keywords. Lateral thinking may help – more practically, you should perform a search yourself, then analyse the pages returned as relevant hits. Keywords can be placed in several places on the page – identifying where they are placed will enable you to build up a set of words and phrases that you can then use in your own pages.

Remember that many of the search indexes use stopwords – those words so common that it is simply not effective to index them or return search results for them. Even if indexed, the sheer volume of results will make it impossible for your site to gain any prominence. Once you have selected your keywords, carry out an Alta Vista search on each keyword in turn. See how many instances are records, and how the top two or three sites have designed their pages to reach the top of the listing. Where have they placed their keywords, and how often on the page do they occur? Use their success as a benchmark for your own page design and promotion.

Avoid the use of single character terms (e.g. vitamin K), terms with foreign accents, and words such as Web, Internet, email, or home which appear in 90% of all Web sites. They will either simply not be matched or else they will be ignored by the index.

Keyword Placement

By definition keywords should reflect and describe the content and subject of your Web page. The presence of the relevant terms in the general body text should ensure that your page is returned as a result for a search. To appear higher in the listings requires a higher 'score' and this results from the keyword appearing more often and more relevantly in the page. Most indexes give higher relevance scores for the following:

- First paragraph
- Heading
- TITLE
- URL
- Frequency
- ALT
- COMMENTS
- META.

First Paragraph

Ensure your keywords appear in the first paragraph of text. Some indexers only include the first 50 or 100 words, some simply give a higher score if the word appears in the first paragraph. Either way, good information design suggests that you should avoid a rambling introduction – start with relevant information, and include the keywords.

Heading

Keywords placed within <H1> tags are assumed to be important. HTML was designed as a means of describing the structure of documents, not their layout and design. The heading tag therefore confirms the importance of a term. Although you can achieve the same display using a FONT command with a SIZE attribute, the significance to the index is greatly reduced.

<TITLE>

Words and phrases placed within the <TITLE> tag will appear in the blue line at the top of the screen, and will be returned in the set of search results as the title of the page. Indexers also generally attach a higher score to keywords placed here, and particularly to the first word or two in longer titles. Many sites simply have the company name as the title on every page – this is very unhelpful, particularly if you expect visitors to bookmark particular areas within your site – the bookmark title is also taken from the <TITLE> tag. There is a trade-off here between visual clues and technical advantage: too many keywords and it looks ridiculous, none at all is a wasted opportunity. 60 characters is generally an acceptable maximum length. The title should be written using your best copy-righting skills – it has to stand out from at least nine other titles on a results list, so should look relevant and interesting, not merely descriptive. The TITLE is a particular problem in sites using FRAMES, as only the TITLE of the FRAMESET page will be displayed unless you have provided an effective NOFRAMES alternative.

URL (Uniform Resource Locator)

Keywords also typically receive a higher score if they are in the URL of the page. This is often not possible to change, but if you are planning a site and have the option between naming a file database.html or 3653-45a.html, choose the former. Alta Vista, for example, allows you to search for words within a URL (using the url:keyword option).

Frequency

In simple terms, the more often a keyword appears in the page, the higher the score. However you could quickly make your page look ridiculous by the unnecessary mentions of particular words, no matter how relevant – *"Welcome to AskAtTheDesk Information service, for all your information needs. If you want information, we have information, well-organised information on all sorts of information-based topics of information"*. You get the point (I hope!). Frequency is not just a question of large numbers. It is also a proportional measure. A shorter page with a few mentions of the keyword will do better than a very long page, even if it has a few more mentions, as the indexer will calculate the percentage of the words on the page that are relevant to the search. More than a certain level, perhaps as low as 3-4% of the content will be interpreted as 'keyword spamming', the deliberate repetition of keywords, and penalised by removing the page from the index.

<ALT>

Most search engines index all the HTML code, so provide an ALT statement for each image. This is good design practice anyway, as it enables those without graphics to understand your page more easily. Instead of just ALT="news" use the space effectively: ALT="news about AskAtTheDesk research services".

<COMMENT>

The comment tag allows the Web page designer to insert statements of ownership or copyright, perhaps to insert reminders as to why a particular style has been used. `<!-- this is a comment -->` will be invisible to the page visitor, but can be read by the indexer (or anyone who views the page's source code, and so offers an opportunity to insert a few well-chosen keywords near to the top of the page. This is particularly useful where the page is composed of a large logo or set of images, limiting the space for text.

<META>

Metadata is the information about the document or page, the equivalent of the cataloguing information for a book. There are several dozen fields that you could use, particularly if your information is going to be indexed by a subject specific database, or one of the developing news services. A limited set of the available field has been developed – the Dublin Core – which provides a standardised set of descriptive fields, such as author, language, publisher etc. Further information on this developing area can be found on UKOLN's Web site (www.ukoln.ac.uk/metadata/), and an example of use can be seen in the NewsAgent for Libraries project (www.sbu.ac.uk/litc/newsagent/).

Two particular options are the Keyword and Description. These are used by several of the largest search engines to identify relevance against searches. The <META> tag in the HTML source code provides the indexing services with the keywords and content descriptions that you choose, rather than the ones they generate automatically. There is capacity to provide a large number of words in the META tags, with search engines varying in the number they accept. However, the repetition of keywords to force a higher score is not acceptable – indeed, some actually penalise repeated words giving you a lower score than might otherwise have been the case. The length of content should not be unnecessarily lengthy – description to 150 characters, keywords to about 750 characters. Different search indexers allow different lengths, but these limits reflect the most widely accepted limits. Place the most important keywords at the start of the list, to provide extra emphasis.

Normally, commas should separate keywords in the META Keyword listing. However, where the word is part of a phrase, use the phrase as another keyword. Although simple repetition is frowned upon, multiple use is not exactly the same thing. For example: information, research, database, database research, research information, information research provides the opportunity for a wide range of searches to score successfully, employing multiple usage whilst avoiding simple repetition.

This is how the HTML code for the head of a typical page might look:

```
<HEAD>

<TITLE>AskAtTheDesk Information: research,
databases, information resources. </TITLE>

<META Name="keywords" Content="relevant, mean-
ingful, numerous, words and phrases, essen-
tial, considered, well-chosen">

<META Name="description" Content="A concise
and meaningful description of the site, that
is presented as a search result.">

</HEAD>
```

Many HTML editing packages (FrontPage, PageMill, HotMetal et al) let you enter the keywords and description as part of the page properties, so you can avoid getting to grips with the raw HTML as above.

Beat the Best

Perform a search using typical keywords relevant to your product or service. Look at the top 10 or 20 results in several of the main search engines. Use the View/Source command in the browser to see what they have put in their META tags, and work out why they are top of the list. Learn, adapt and improve. Alternatively, use the Meta Tag Analyzer from *Scrub The Web* (www.scrubtheweb.com/abs/meta-check.html), which will go to your page and check your title, keyword and description entries, suggesting improvements where necessary.

A recent report from Web Site Garage (www.fullsitetuneup.com) showed that the majority of sites who use the service have not made full use of the potential: 7.1% of sites have not used <TITLE> in their source code, 60.8% have not used <META keyword> and 58.8% have not used <META description>. These are not secrets, nor are they difficult features, but they are something that many Web site designers overlook – at their peril.

Repeat Indexing

Over time, many sites' position on the search engines will degrade – better-designed sites are indexed and priority may be given to newer sites. It is important to maintain the attention of the indexing software where possible, particularly if you are adding content to your pages that you wish to be found. By adding an instruction within the <META> tags, you can pull the spidering software back to your site. Place this snippet of HTML code within your <HEAD> tags on key pages:

```
<META NAME= "revisit-after" CONTENT="15 days">
<META NAME="ROBOTS" CONTENT="ALL">
```

JavaScript

If you have JavaScript placed in your <HEAD>, make sure that all the <META> tags are before the <JAVASCRIPT> tag. Some indexers will either try to index the JavaScript code, or simply leave the <HEAD> section, skipping your <META> tags completely.

Use the Opportunity

Many site designers simply copy the HEAD section of a page, using it as a template for all subsequent pages. This means that the KEYWORDS and DESCRIPTIONS are the same throughout a site, and frequently the TITLE as well. This is missing the whole point of these tags. They should describe the page to which they are attached. If they are all the same, they can only respond to one range of search terms. If they vary throughout the site, then the range of searches for which some part of your site might be retrieved is correspondingly widened. At the very least, the top page of each section or directory should have a distinct and relevant set of keywords and description. These pages can then be submitted separately, improving your presence on the search indexes.

The Unique Keyword

One powerful and effective method for assessing how your sites have progressed in being indexed is to insert a unique keyword in to your <META> tags. Mix letters and numbers to ensure that it won't occur anywhere else – use a term like **'tagtesting'** and transpose some letters and numbers, making it into **ta6t35t1ng**. Place it on each page you produce, or at least on each page you submit for indexing, and then perform a search in AltaVista. The number of results will be exactly the number of your pages in that index.

Specific Search Engine Requirements

Who is all this work for?

Search indexes vary. Some, like Alta Vista, InfoSeek and HotBot support <META> tags. Others, such as Excite, reason that as you can lie in the <META> tags, it is better for them to index the actual content of the page. So design with both approaches in mind.

Frames

Indexing robots cannot access framed Web sites unless there is a <NOFRAMES> alternative, because the framed home page has no links leading in to your site, just the <FRAMESET> layout. As with <ALT> attributes, the use of <NOFRAMES> is good helpful design – ignore them at your peril.

Maintenance

Just as you should not abandon your Web pages once they are published, so the same applies for the search engine listings. Re-submission every 3-6 months will allow you to update the index – new content, new keywords, new position on the results listings.

The Top Search Services

The search services listed below probably account for over 90% of Web searching activity. The effort spent submitting your site to each of these will be repaid by a significant presence of your information service on the most important indexes and directories in this medium. The time taken for the services to add your site after submission varies from a day or two to several weeks. It may then take further submissions and perhaps revisiting your keywords and even page content to ensure that you optimise your positioning on these databases.

Many of these indexes and directories supply the data for other branded services. Submitting to the other services may prove quicker, as they are often a subset of the information in the parent database, with faster overall indexing speeds. Sites included in the branded service will be automatically included in the parent database, thus providing a 'back door': this applies particularly to UKPlus and Yahoo!UK.

Excite

www.excite.com
50 million documents
Global Index
Submitting to Excite also gets your site on Netscape Search and AOL NetFind. Shorter URLs rank higher than long URLs (implies higher level page). <META> tags are not indexed, but description displayed in results. Excite derives keywords from

first few sentences. TITLE is even more important as META Keywords are ignored; <NOFRAMES> needed. Excite owns Magellan and WebCrawler.

InfoSeek

www.InfoSeek.com
30 million documents
Global Index
Submission should result in listing within 2-3 days. Use lower case only in <META> keywords. <META> tags important; all words indexed, stemming supported; <NOFRAMES> needed; <COMMENTS> and <ALT> tags indexed. Pages should be retrievable within 48 hours of submission. Maximum submissions 25 pages per day. The InfoSeek database is used by UKPlus (www.ukplus.co.uk) and Search.Com (www.search.com), to which submissions should also be made.

Alta Vista

www.altavista.com
150 million documents
Global Index
<NOFRAMES> useful; <TITLE>, <META> and <ALT> tags important. Longer documents can perform better in the index, as can older documents. Indexing only goes 'down' two or three levels – wide, flatter sites are therefore better indexed. Submitting the same page more than once a month is penalised, as is submitting more than five pages per day. Alta

Vista's database serves the LookSmart directory (www.looksmart.com), and is an option on Yahoo!.

Lycos

www.Lycos.com
32 million pages
Global Index
Include at least 100 words of text to be indexed favourably – keywords and phrases should represent about 1-2% of the total word count. Priority also goes to home and directory pages (those named index.html). <NOFRAMES> needed; stemming supported. <META> and <ALT> tags are indexed, but are just treated as ordinary text. Lycos also runs the *Top 5%* service.

HotBot

www.HotBot.com
115 million
Global Index
Submitting to HotBot also gets your site into MSN Search. <NOFRAMES> needed; <!COMMENTS> indexed; <META> tags important. Powered by the Inktomi search engine which also powers Yahoo! and Snap (www.snap.com).

WebCrawler

www.webcrawler.com
2 million
Global Index
Owned by Excite, but operated as an independent search engine. <TITLE> and regular occurrence of keywords crucial. Links back to the main page from each submitted page are vital in the scoring process. The first full text search service, but has been overtaken by the big players.

Search UK

www.searchuk.com
3 million (target 95% .uk pages)
UK-specific Index
Speed of entry: Submitted sites are added to database within 4-6 weeks. All Web sites outside the .uk domain are checked by humans to ensure they are indeed UK sites. Relevance criteria: "Weighting is given to various factors. We advise people to think how we, as humans, determine meaning from a page, and to apply that to their web page." <META> tags supported.

Euroferret

www.euroferret.com
34 million (specifically European)
European Index
Indexes only European domains, so .com and .net won't be accepted. The indexer analyses the structure of each document, extracting the 60 most important words and 12 key phrases to index on.

Analysing structure means that <TITLE> and <H1> tags are prioritised. Medium length documents packed with keywords may thus do better here.

Northern Light

www.northernlight.com
65 million pages, 5,500 special sources
Global Index
Maximum 120 submissions per user per day, requests only top level page submitted for crawling. Claims to index every word or every page of every Web site. Much favoured by information professionals because of its ability to create topic folders on the fly from results lists, plus access to special collections (at a fee).

Guerilla Marketing

Guerilla Marketing applied to the Web is a concept that first appeared in a 1984 book of the same name by Jay Conrad Levinson. He defines it as "achieving conventional goals, such as profits and joy, with unconventional methods, such as investing energy instead of money".

Theoretically it provides a way in which small sites can achieve visibility despite their lack of advertising or marketing budgets, using low-cost methods. Guerilla marketing is "simple to understand, easy to implement and outrageously inexpensive". Effectively a series of tips, hints and tricks that achieve good results, the original concept has been subverted by those who use 'dirty tricks' campaigns to get their Web site noticed. Ethically dubious, these techniques in effect force a search engine to return a false result, e.g. list a Web site far higher up the rankings than its content would imply it has a right to be.

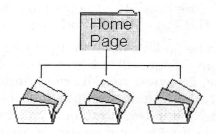

Conventional Home Page

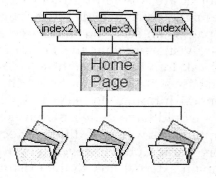

Using Alternative Home Pages

Diagram 3. Alternative Home pages

Duplicate 'Front Doors' or 'Bridges'

This is, in my opinion, the one acceptable guerilla marketing tactic. The duplicate front door or bridge page is a Web page whose keywords focus on a specific feature or topic of the site, with appropriate keywords both as <META> tags and as text on the page, and either with a single link to your home page, or a replicated set of links to the next level. Indeed, there is no reason why these pages should not be exact replicas of the home page, but with different <TITLE>, <META> and <ALT> content.

There need be no links back to these pages, as all pages within the site will link back to the 'genuine' home page, i.e. **www.yoursite.co.uk/index.html**. The replica home pages might then be called **index2.html** and **index3.html** for simplicity's sake. This is then submitted and indexed, capturing hits for a specific subject area. This is ideal if you have several subject areas – getting them all into the home page might look unwieldy, so creating a range of special pages can score on the search engines, leading extra visitors to your site. So, for example, AskAtTheDesk Information might have one page for the Database service, one for Research and one for the general Information Service. Each of the three pages would have quite different keywords and descriptions, as well as a different focus in its introductory paragraph. However, they would all have one main external link to the existing home page of the company. Submitted separately, these pages should thus pick up enquiries in the different specialties of the company. No false keywords, no misleading descriptions, just an opportunity to focus attention on core areas.

These may not win you any design awards, but they may raise your site a few notches in the results lists of the leading search engines. More importantly, they may enable your site to be the result for a wider range of search queries. After all, if you can't be found, you might as well not be there.

Although for illustrative purposes I have suggested above you might call the other pages **index2.html**, **index3.html** etc, you will achieve far more by using the opportunity to name them significantly: **database.html**, **research.html** and so on. Keywords appearing in the URL score highly in the indexing.

There are a number of other practices which you may hear about – hidden text, invisible GIFs (Graphic Interchange Format) and keyword spamming. The search engines are increasingly wise to these practices. Trying these techniques may be tempting, but be warned – you are actually more likely to move down the rankings than up, as most indexes actively penalise sites which use these tricks.

- *Hidden Text*

Very small text at the top or bottom of your page, in the same colour as the background, containing your keywords. They will be invisible to visitors, but hope to be indexed by the search engine as part of the main text.

- *Invisible Images*

Similar to the above suggestion, several one pixel-square GIFs (set to be transparent, and therefore invisible against the background page colour), each with the ALT text containing the relevant keywords. These hope to be read by the indexing robot, adding to your page's relevance score.

- *Deliberately False Keywords*

This involves placing the name of a competitor in your keyword list, to attract visitors who were searching for another site, or placing high-usage search terms (Titanic, Microsoft, sex, football etc.) in to the <META Keyword> of an information site. This may cause your site to be returned as the result for a search – but you would be unlikely to impress the searcher – quite apart from the effect this might have on your manager and your professional credibility. For example, many sex sites used 'Superbowl 98' as a keyword (so I read recently), presumably on the grounds that American Football fans had much in common with their target audience. Apart from being generally libellous, for all but the most careless site manager this is a very high-risk strategy. Do not do it.

- *Keyword Spamming*

Indexing tools often ignore repeated words, but if you alternate them, or repeat them in a cycle of four or five words, you may raise the score without being penalised. Also deliberately overloading the visible text with keywords, apart from looking and reading strangely, may be penalised as indexes look for a 'sensible' ratio of keywords to body text (perhaps as low as 2-3%.

• *<META refresh> Tags*

Creating differing home pages that refresh or refer the visitor instantly to the real front page. The speed of the change may make it invisible to the visitor, but the hope is that the indexer will pick up another set of keywords.

Let me be very clear: do *not* use these techniques. They will almost always be penalised by the indexes. If you see them used on another site, permit yourself a wry smile at the site designer's naiveté, or be outraged at their deceptive manner.

Testing Your Success

Once you have put in the design effort, and followed the advice in the next chapter, on Submitting Your Site, you need to measure the success – or otherwise – of your efforts. There are a number of ways in which this can be done.

• *Manual testing*

Search for your site in the search engines to which you have submitted. Keep going through the results until you find your pages. Note the position on a chart, along with the date. Improve your page design. Re-submit. Repeat the process until satisfied.

• *Web-based services*

Using a free service such as RankThis (www.rankthis.com), you can find out quickly whether your site is in the top 200 results in a search of any of 12 search services. A more comprehensive service is offered by PositionAgent (www.positionagent.com), which monitors your site's position in the top ten search engines, and delivers the report to your desktop. This is not a free service, but may be highly cost effective if you have revenue-based targets to achieve from your Web site. More details on these two services are provided in Chapter 9, *Monitoring and Measurement*.

- *Software-based services*

WebPosition (www.webposition.com) software will perform the same task as RankThis, but in more depth, covering a wider range of keywords and phrases. Freely downloadable, this software may become a useful monitoring tool.

Whichever method you use, attempt to maintain a record of your success and visibility in the search result – if you can't find your own site, then it's likely that others can't either. In which case, you'll need to go back to the top results, and see how they have achieved their success.

References

Levinson, Jay Conrad. *Guerilla Marketing* (London: Piatkus, 1994).

4. URL Submission

The previous chapter described the design techniques needed to make this chapter's activity successful. Although the large search indexes do search the Web automatically for pages to add to their index, they can only do this by following links from page to page. If your site is new, or obscure, or simply not very well known, there may be few, if any, inbound links from other sites. To ensure that you appear in these search services, it is therefore essential that you take the initiative and actively submit your site for indexing and inclusion.

This is welcomed by the search services themselves, because their financial success depends on size. They exist by advertising revenue, which depends on visitors. If they are to compete, they have to appear comprehensive, as well as fast, effective and easy to use.

Ideally you would feature in every database, but there are over 2,000 currently in operation. In practice the top six or seven account for some 80% of searching activity, so focus on them first, dealing with others in batches as your resources and inclination permit. The list below combines those generally accepted to be the best (i.e. largest, busiest) with some more specific sites that are worth submitting to:

Global Indexes	**UK & European Indexes**
Alta Vista	Euroferret
HotBot	UKPlus
InfoSeek	Search UK
Excite	GOD
Northern Light	
Lycos	**UK Directories**
WebCrawler	
OpenText	UK Index
Magellan	UK Directory

Directories	**Online Newsletters**
Yahoo! , Yahoo! UK	Internet Resource Newsletter
LookSmart	FreePint
MiningCo	
BUBL	

Portals

Many of the search indexes are now becoming Web portals. A portal is a hybrid news, directory and index that aims to be your starting point for all Web activities. With search indexes that also offer directories you have two avenues for promotion – the keyword search and the directory drill-down. A drill-down is where the user enters a directory at the top level and follows the menus through the various sub-directories, drilling down until eventually – hopefully – they end up at a link to your site.

UK Versions

As the Web continues to develop, many of the search services are localising their content. InfoSeek,

Excite and Yahoo! all have UK versions of their service, with locally-based staff and servers, providing easier access to UK-specific content. It can be easier to achieve a higher position on these services, simply because they are smaller than the parent global site. Additionally, the fact that they have dedicated resources for the local service means that they can respond quicker to listing requests for UK sites. The bonus is that sites added to the local version also get added to the global service, providing an accessible entry route.

Top Search Engine Sites

Search Engine	% Reach
yahoo.com	46.0
excite.com	25.8
InfoSeek.com	24.8
Alta Vista	20.9
Lycos.com	19.9
HotBot.com	5.8
looksmart.com	5.1
webcrawler.com	5.0
snap.com	4.9
goto.com	4.9

Media Metrix (www.mediametrix.com) report of % Reach for Search Services August 1998

The figure for "%Reach" means that 46% of surveyed users have used Yahoo!, 25.8% have used Excite etc. This was a survey of business users, and so the results may vary somewhat for academic or personal users.

Yahoo!

Yahoo! is easily the most important general site on which to be listed. There are certainly subject-specific sites that are more relevant for particular sectors, but for sheer weight of numbers, Yahoo! remains the most important directory by far. However, Yahoo! differs from the other leading search services in several respects.

Firstly it is a directory, not an index. This means that the structure of the content is very different, being held in a hierarchical set of directories and sub-directories through which the user navigates, drilling down several layers to reach the required information. Secondly, although there is a search tool on the Yahoo! site, it is not a full-text keyword search – it is a catalogue search. In other words, what you are searching is the bibliographic record relating to a particular site, not the full text of the content of that site. Thirdly, links are to sites, not specific pages. Links almost invariably take you to the home page of a site, from where you have to follow the links to the information. In indexes, you are taken straight to the relevant page. Fourth, it is compiled by humans, not by computer. This makes it less predictable, and potentially much slower, as a means of adding your information to the database. Fifth, which follows on from the previous point, sites are reviewed for quality before being added. Up to 50% of sites submitted to Yahoo! are simply not added to the database, perhaps because of bad design, poor content or inappropriate selection of subject area.

Being accepted for inclusion in Yahoo!'s database therefore requires extra effort and persistence; however the resulting traffic means that most Web designers regard it as a price worth paying. Although they won't get a poor site accepted – the quality threshold will still have to be met – there is one key way in which the process can be accelerated. This is to submit your site through a localised Yahoo! such as Yahoo! UK rather than the parent site. Because there is less pressure, acceptance times are generally shorter. The same applies to the twelve U.S. city-specific Yahoo!s, under the Yahoo! Get Local link.

Yahoo!

www.yahoo.com
700,000 sites (not *pages*)
Global Directory
Can take up to 6 weeks to be added to Yahoo!, although Yahoo! UK should be two or three times as quick. It is a directory, not an index, so searches only match keywords against description and title of site as submitted by Yahoo!'s form. Submit only the top level of a site or major directory, as Yahoo! is a site listing service, *not* an index. Submission is through a form on the page in which you would like to be listed. Yahoo! does not accept listings on free site providers (GeoCities, Tripod etc). Listings are sorted alphabetically – *Aardvark Information* may be a better choice of name than *ZsaZsa Research . . .*

And Also Worthy of Note:

Pinakes

Gateway directory
http://www.hw.ac.uk/libWWW/irn/pinakes/
pinakes.html
Not in itself a search service, but a convenient point of access to 33 top subject gateways, many produced as eLib (Electronic Libraries programme) projects. Based on largely academic topics, whichever directory is appropriate for your activity is where you should be included. Submissions should be direct to the subject directories as per their instructions for inclusion.

The Mining Company

Gateway directory
http://www.miningco.com/
More structured gateway directory than Pinakes, aiming to compete ultimately with Yahoo! with over 500 directories managed by subject specialists. Submission is by email to the directory owner – a more personal approach is required.

Other Listings Sites

There are a number of directory listings sites which will accept all relevant submissions – UK Directory (www.ukdirectory.com) and UK Index (www.ukindex.co.uk) for example. Yahoo! is more selective. Lists of these localised directories can be found through the Yahoo! structure, and may be sector or country specific.

What's New/Cool

Submit your URL to the various What's New and What's Cool listings (if you think it is New or Cool, that is). Featuring on one of these can dramatically increase the visitor rate, although submission does not guarantee inclusion – your idea of cool has to match with the definition held by a Californian web expert (allegedly).

Submitting Services

These services will do the submitting for you, with varying effectiveness. The really effective service is paid for of course, but the free services may be worth using as a starting point. However one of the main drawbacks to the free automated tools is that they rarely take account of differences between the different requirements of the search engines. One may require a description of no more than 12 words, another may allow a longer description.

Easy Submit
http://www.scrubtheweb.com/abs/promo.html

Submit-it!
http://www.submit-it.com/

Broadcaster
http://www.broadcaster.co.uk/

Creating the Time-saving Text File

When submitting to search indexes or directories, you will normally need to complete an online form. Most will ask for the same information, so it makes sense to prepare this in advance – this will save time in the long run, and ensure you provide a consistent description of your site. Keep the information as a text file, ready to copy and paste in to submission forms – and make sure that it is updated.

The information you need will typically include:

- a brief description of your site in 15, 25 and 50 words;
- the URL of the page(s) you are submitting;
- a set of keywords;
- name of your site;
- name of your organisation;
- contact name;
- contact email address;
- address and telephone/fax numbers;
- target audience or sector for your product or service.

Not all services require all of these details, but most require at least some of them. Having them to hand will save you time and effort in the long run – particularly if you intend to resubmit to a range of services on a monthly or bimonthly basis.

5. Establishing Links

Reciprocal Links

A 'related links' page adds value to your site: increase the benefit by requesting the owners of linked sites to place a return link on their pages. Remember that this is a favour, not an obligation. You cannot insist, but if you can show that the content on your site is of direct relevance to their visitors (and is not in direct competition), then it is often mutually beneficial to link the two sites. Links to and from sites that themselves have high traffic and good links pages will improve the traffic flow for your site. If chosen well, they should also attract qualified and motivated visitors who are actively searching for the information or service that you provide.

The relative size of your organisation and its activity may affect the success of this tactic – a local wine merchant (or enthusiast) might have a link to Tesco's wine ordering service or the Chateau Lafitte Web site: expecting a reciprocal link might be a little optimistic. Similarly many small information services will have links to, say, the British Library without any realistic expectation of a return link. National institutions apart, the most useful sites to which to link to will be those that provide good content, or access to good content. If your Web site contains useful content, then by definition they will want to link to you . . . perhaps.

You should avoid offering a link to another site only if they link to you. Either they are good enough to link to or they are not. This should be an entirely separate issue from a link request, although an existing link from your site should be a good sign from their point of view.

Make It Easy

The easier you make it, the more chance there is that a relevant site will link back to you. Create a page, with the HTML code visible for the link text. Then all the other site has to do is copy and paste that code in to their own page. You might also create a standard-sized button and banner, again providing the relevant code to be copied. When you email a potential link site, include the code in the body of the email, and provide a reference to the page where the images can be copied, as in the illustration below.

Targeted emails to the owners of related sites can be very effective. Start with some praise for their Web site, explain the relevance of yours, and conclude with an invitation to link.

```
Dear Site Owner,

I recently found your excellent site, and
would like to invite you to link to the
AskAtTheDesk site. I think our services would
be of interest to your site's visitors, and I
would be happy to place a link on our related
links page to your site.

To insert the link please copy the following
code:

<a href="http://www.askatthedesk.co.uk"><img
src="http://www.askatthedesk.co.uk/graphics/
```

```
button.gif" border=0 height=40 width=80
alt="AskAtTheDesk Information Services"></a>
```

or for a simple text link:

```
<a href="http://
www.askatthedesk.co.uk">AskAtTheDesk Informa-
tion Services</a>
```

Many thanks,

AskAtTheDesk Information Services

http://www.askatthedesk.co.uk/

Most leading search engines now provide a page where you can copy and paste the code for their dialogue box into your pages, to enable your visitors to start a search from your page. They do this for a very simple reason: the easier it is to do, the more people will do it. It is a useful service to your site, but their motive is simple – money. Their revenue is based on advertising. The more visitors they can encourage the more their advertisers like it – and the more they pay.

The same principle applies to your site, whether revenue is at stake or not. The easier you make it, the more likely it is that links will be created to your site. Links generate site traffic, and more importantly perhaps, they generate traffic from sites of related interest. In other words, the visitors you get will be interested in your subject area, product or service.

Directory Links

It can be useful to spend some time working through your own bookmark list to see which are the gateway resources in your sector, and what links they have on their site – and whether you should be included. Clearly your target audience will be interested in these sites, so it is important for your site to be visible there where possible. Professional bodies, trade associations, research consortia, subject gateways – all should be high on your list for requesting links.

Contacting the appropriate email and usenet discussion groups may also be a useful starting point in identifying likely prospects, whilst of course observing the conventions of the group. Uninvited and inappropriate messages may have a negative outcome, but used carefully these groups of interested professionals could provide access to a useful collection of linking sites. Perhaps even a polite 'naive' message asking for advice on useful sites to link to might generate some useful and positive suggestions.

WebRing (www.webring.com)

A structured system of reciprocal links which allows web sites with similar interest to form "rings" of sites, allowing visitors a fast and efficient way to find content, is a useful way for sites to build traffic and gain exposure.

Over 18,000 rings link nearly a quarter of a million sites. A minimum of five like-minded sites is required to start a ring. Each site then adds a link at the bottom of their page, which takes the visitor to the 'next' site in the ring. Alternatively the visitor can go to a list of the next 5 sites, or a list of all the sites in a ring, and choose the route for him or herself. As a Web site manager, you might seek a ring to join, or you might decide to set up a ring for information sites in your sector. One potentially profitable strategy is to join or start a ring where the other members are already high-traffic sites. This way you gain benefit from their existing high profile. The key aim after all is to gain a net inflow of traffic.

LoopLink (http://www.looplink.com)

Broadly similar in concept to WebRing, LoopLink offers a more quality-controlled approach, with only 70 rings and 2,000 sites, most of which are commercial, all of which are pre-screened and continually checked.

Active Encouragement

Bookmarks and Links are two sides of the same coin. A bookmark is simply a link stored on the visitor's computer, easily accessible, and as such it should generate repeat visits on a regular basis. Encouraging your visitors to bookmark your site, and providing the simple instructions, means that the chances that they will return are increased. Of course some people simply collect enormous bookmark lists and then never revisit the pages listed, but the results should justify the small effort involved in adding a brief text page to the site. It might look something like the outline below:

Bookmark This Site

If you want to make sure you can always get to where you want to - AskAtTheDesk - then be sure to bookmark AskAtTheDesk or add us to your Favourites. You can press **control-D** to do this with most browsers. Alternatively, you can use the following methods:

Netscape Users - You should see the following
menu options at the top of your Netscape
screen: File, Edit, View, Go, Bookmarks...etc.
Click on Bookmarks and then click on Add Bookmark. That's it! Next time you want to get
somewhere you want to in AskAtTheDesk, you can
simply go to the Bookmarks menu and click on
AskAtTheDesk.

Microsoft Internet Explorer Users - You should
see the following menu options at the top of
your screen: File, Edit, View,
Favourites...etc. Click on Favourites and then
click on Add To Favourites, now you should see
a requester pop up. Click on the Add button
near the lower right hand corner of the requester. That's it! Next time you want to get
somewhere you want to in AskAtTheDesk, you can
simply go to the Favourites menu and click on
AskAtTheDesk.

If you use another browser, please use the
online help to use the bookmark service.

Measuring Progress

Keep a chart or spreadsheet listing those sites to
which you have sent link requests, as well as
those that have requested links from you to them.
You can search to identify sites which have links
to you: HotBot offers an option in the drop-down
menu, and on Alta Vista you should use the
search dialogue:

+www.yoursite.ac.uk
-url:www.yoursite.ac.uk

which searches for all instances of your URL ex-
cept for those on your own site. You should also
check the referrers listed in your site statistical re-
ports, if you have access to the server logs that de-
tail all visitors to your site. Plotting the growth in

the number of inbound links should provide a rising curve – if not, you have work to do. Listing the email address of the site manager of each linked site gives you a specialised mailing list that will be useful for announcing new features on your site: you may be able to negotiate special announcements or joint promotional activities, for example.

6. Email Interactivity and Permission Marketing

One of the key features of the Internet as a communications medium is the interactivity it provides. The more interactivity built into a site, the greater the relationship that develops between the site and its audience. The visitor is not just a recipient of the message. There can – and should – be a dialogue between the visitor and the Web site: feedback, queries, orders, varying pathways, database interaction, games, personalisation of content – all these features make the experience something greater than just reading text on a screen. And the better the experience, the more likely a visitor is to return. This is relationship marketing – creating a two-way flow of communication that adds value to the visit.

Interaction can be built into a Web site in a number of ways, for example by publishing content dynamically from a database, or by providing online calculating tools that can be queried – or by using one or more of the various email tools available. The intention here is both to build new traffic and encourage repeat visits. The tools and services outlined below are free – some insert banner adverts which may be avoided by buying the 'pro' version. Alternatively you may have the technical skills or resources to write scripts yourself to carry out these tasks. Using the free services is normally as simple as filling out a Web-based form, then setting a few parameters before being provided with a link or some HTML code to insert into your pages.

A new concept – or at least a new piece of jargon – is 'permission marketing' or 'opt-in'. Most Internet users dislike and resent junk email, or 'spam'. Sending out unwanted emails can often have a negative marketing outcome. This is avoided by inviting visitors to opt-in, in other words to volunteer to join a mailing list or discussion. If the newsletter arrives as the result of a positive decision, it is far more likely to hit the target than if it is sent out at random, or to those whose address you have acquired by other means. If you sign up registered visitors to a list, make it very clear that this is what will happen.

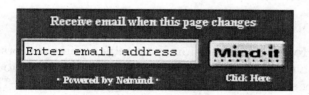

Interactive Email Marketing Tools

URL Minder (www.netmind.com)

For pages whose content changes significantly, inserting a URL Minder form can act as a useful prompt for a return visit. This free service sends a three or four line email notifying the subscriber that a page they are interested in has changed, and provides the URL. Using a service such as this is more appropriate for pages where the content changes significantly, but only occasionally, for example on a Press Release page, a list of services, or perhaps prices or opening times. On a page which changes daily, the resulting daily email would be an irritant rather than a useful reminder. NetMind provides the HTML code, as with several of the tools.

Copy and paste the code provided to create this simple form: your visitors get added value, and a

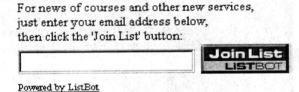

For news of courses and other new services, just enter your email address below, then click the 'Join List' button:

Powered by ListBot

reminder to return when you update the page's content.

Discussion List

Hosting a discussion list enables your visitors to share common queries, perhaps act as a user group, or simply as a network of like-minded visitors. This can be used to discuss advanced features of your service, or as a means of discussing problems, new releases and additions, or service breaks. Discussion list management software such as Majordomo (www.greatcircle.com/majordomo/) is widely available, at no cost. Maintaining your own email discussion list software gives you complete control over list policies and membership. Alternatively, in the higher education sector, discussion lists can be set up and operated through the Mailbase service (www.mailbase.ac.uk), as long as a significant proportion of the members are in the academic domain. Another option is to use Web-based services such as ListBot (www.listbot.com) or MakeList (www.makelist.com), which provide a free list hosting service, suitable for most purposes.

All the Web visitor need do is supply an email address to be added to a newsletter list, or to be emailed full instructions on how to participate in the discussion list.

Newsletter

The same software that runs discussion lists can be used to deliver newsletters. By changing the settings so that only the list-owner (i.e. you) can send messages, your visitors can be invited to sign up to a newsletter service that keeps them informed about changes and additions to your services. A monthly newsletter with one or two useful pointers, tips and announcements helps to keep your service uppermost in the mind of the site visitors. Special events, competitions or other newsworthy items can be promoted in this way, and are successful and popular.

MailMe (www.mailme.co.uk)

MailMe is a tool developed by the Royal Mail to provide enquirers with fast access to product or service information at the touch of a button.

Downloadable from the Royal Mail Web site, the MailMe software helps you set up interactive forms which capture customer information and initiate a pre-determined action – for example the despatch of an information pack. This free tool adds simplicity to the task of requesting information, meaning that visitors get access to the information they need quickly and easily.

ReferMe (deadlock.com/refer/)

Add a form to the most useful pages within your Web site, inviting visitors to let their friends and colleagues know about your wonderful resource. The visitor might be inclined to do this anyway of course, but this makes the whole process as simple as clicking on a button and entering an email address . . . or a few. This form lets you recruit your visitors as site promoters in your behalf. You could create a script to do this yourself, or go to Deadlock Design's Web site where you can let them do all the work (automatically) for you – and it's free.

Signature Files

Virtually all email packages allow you to specify a signature file. This is a plain text file stored on your PC. Whenever you send a message, this is added at the end automatically. Adding a useful signature file to your email (and ensuring everyone in the department or organisation does likewise) means that each message acts as a small promotional bonus; a one-line advert or description, with URL, email and address is typical.

```
============================================================
John  Smith                                  Information
Information  Services                          Resources
AskAtTheDesk  Information  Ltd                  Databases
1 Main Street,  Anytown.
Tel:  01234  567890 Email:smith@askatthedesk.co.uk
Fax:01234  567891 http://www.askatthedesk.co.uk/
============================================================
```

Example email signature

7. Press Releases and Notification

There is a large body of trade, professional and general media who need to fill their column inches each issue with information of interest and relevance to their readership or subscribers. A well-designed press release can be a boon to the hard-pressed journalist approaching deadlines with space to fill. Simply sending out a badly designed press release is potentially damaging – not only do you miss an opportunity for positive coverage or attention, you may actually diminish the value of your site in the eyes of professionally-qualified commentators. This is particularly the case in the trade and professional media where the recipient, if not actually expert, will at least recognise key features of the relevant sector.

An Action Checklist

To ensure that your press release does your site the best possible service, apply some or all of the following suggestions – some are golden rules, others simply good practice, all bear careful consideration.

1. Send the release to a named person, ideally the editor or writer of the section in which you hope to feature, and only to one person per publication.

2. Give enough time prior to the launch of the site, and more importantly before the publi-

cation date: days for a daily, a week or more for a weekly, and at least a month in advance for a monthly publication. Many journals go to press as much as a month before they are actually printed and delivered. Request publication schedules of publications to which you are going to send material more than once.

3. Keep the release short and to the point, in a newsy style. A headline should provide the one key point in plain English. Leave it to the journalist to create a witty pun.

4. The first paragraph particularly should have short sentences, covering the salient points, any of which might provide or inspire a headline. Add a quotation or two where relevant. This provides enough for a busy writer to convert into a story that looks like one written by personal interview.

5. Produce the release on headed paper with a heading proclaiming its status as a Press Release, along with a date of release (and embargo if relevant). Add full contact details at the end, to enable a follow-up call from the recipient, and include a one-paragraph outline of your service or organisation.

6. Add press releases to your Web site – writers proactively monitoring developments may prefer to go where they can copy and paste the text off the screen – and make this availability explicitly clear on the printed release. If it's important enough to send out, it's important enough to add to the Web site! In-

deed, you can make the journalist's life even easier by placing a 'Media Information' button prominently on your home page – even if only temporarily during a launch period.

7.   Remember the journalist's checklist: Who, What, When, Where, Why, How.

8.   Don't forget to explain how the new or redesigned Web site is going to improve the service from the customer's perspective.

9.   One page – two at most. And do not forget the URL – in a prominent place, and in bold typeface.

And things to avoid:

1.   Frequent press releases announcing unimportant events – you don't want to make your releases synonymous with wastepaper!

2.   Jargon should be minimised, even in trade or professional publications – unless crucial, and then a full glossary explanation should be provided (of the two or three unavoidable terms – not a full dictionary).

3.   Quoting third parties without their permission – or even their awareness. Remember they may not relish being cited unexpectedly as your best client.

4.   Exclamation marks! Especially multiple exclamation marks!! It looks unprofessional!!!

5.   If sending out the release by email, don't send attachments, and ensure that it is sent to appropriate addresses or lists – and worded to avoid sounding like a sales pitch: the email press release needs to be seen as useful information, not a blatant advertisement.

Announcements

Active and appropriate participation in Usenet newsgroups or Email discussion lists can keep your name uppermost in your audience's mind. This may not reach clients immediately, but by becoming a familiar name to your sector colleagues you will raise the profile of your Web site – and thence your service. You can conduct a search for newsgroups using the DejaNews search service (www.dejanews.com), using the keywords that you will be using in your Web pages <META> tags. Similarly, a search through likely email discussion lists can be carried out using Liszt (www.liszt.com).

Caution is a requirement here – newsgroups and discussion lists are generally unreceptive to blatant advertising. Reading previous postings in the archives will tell you when or if announcements and marketing messages are welcomed, or even permitted by the members. Any promotional message is best dressed up a little either as a response to a query – which requires some patience to make it appropriate to members of specific groups, or submitted with courtesy as an information service to colleagues.

PR Launch

The launch or significant extension of your Web site is a good general marketing opportunity – press releases about an event, not just about the Web site as detailed earlier in this chapter, should be sent to existing and prospective customers, the relevant trade or professional media, suppliers, trade associations and advice groups active in your area. It also provides an opportunity to invite your users to visit your physical location, and explore other uses of the service.

News Media

All the quality newspapers now have a technology or Internet supplement once a week. Each of these carries a few short notices or reviews of recently launched Web sites or services. You may need to prove that your site has something extra – that elusive factor X – to be included, but it is worth notifying the relevant columnist for the exposure to an internet-friendly audience.

The Broadsheet Supplements

Sunday	**Sunday Times**	*Innovations*
Monday	**Independent**	*Network*
Wednesday	**Times**	*Interface*
Thursday	**Telegraph**	*Connected*
Thursday	**Guardian**	*OnLine*

The *Financial Times* also has a regular Internet column.

Internet Media

The general Internet magazines also carry large numbers of site reviews and brief new items. Again, as with any press release, yours will need to be relevant, interesting and possibly just a little different:

- *Internet Magazine*
- *.Net*
- *Internet World*

- *Internet Works*
- *Internet Business*

These publications are of course also a good source of ideas for design and promotion – see what the market leaders are up to and improve on it or adapt it to your specific sector.

Library and Information Media

Press Releases feature prominently in the sources for news in brief in a number of professional publications. Although more specialist media will be for you to research, the general information sector media are also useful sources of potential publicity: *Managing Information, Library Technology, Information World Review* and the Institute of Information Scientists' *Update* are among the most widely read and informative in this area. Many of the special interest groups of the Library Association, the Institute of Information Scientists and Aslib publish newsletters and their own Web sites, to which your site might be added to mutual benefit.

Associations, Institutes and Organisations

Almost every activity has a range of organisations devoted to supporting and informing members about news, trends and developments in the relevant area. The information sector alone has many dozens of such associations, from small special interest groups to national and international groups with tens of thousands of members. Newsletters, journals and electronic media are all profitable targets for your announcements. Bodies active in your specialist area can be found in the *British Directory of Associations* and also in *The Aslib Directory of Information Sources in the United Kingdom*, now in its 10th edition. This last title now includes Web and email addresses in its entries, so if your information service is included, ensure that you use this opportunity to get further publicity for your site.

Print Still Matters!

Add the URL and email to all your printed materials: stationery, printed advertising, invoices, orders, internal memos, business cards, brochures etc. And ensure that all staff – especially the switchboard operator – are aware of the details. It is as surprising how many Web pages lack telephone numbers and addresses as it is that much printed stationery and advertising lacks email and Web addresses.

Internal Promotion

Everyone who deals with your organisation should be aware that there is information available on your Web site. They should have a general idea of what is available, and of course they need to know how to access it. This applies to all stakeholders – staff and management, clients and suppliers. Word of mouth provides effective marketing, and your entire stakeholder community should be recruited to spread the word. Recent surveys in the Internet media suggest that the vast majority of telephone switchboards in larger organisations are unaware of that organisation's Web and email details. A memo or postcard circulated from top to bottom of the organisation may help avoid this apparent invisibility.

And Back Online . . .

There are several Web directory and listing services provided by the UK information sector, which can ensure a wider coverage of appropriate Web sites. Submission to these may not guarantee a great volume of visits, but it will ensure that they are placed in front of a wide range of information professionals.

Internet Resources Newsletter

http://www.hw.ac.uk/libWWW/irn/irn.html
A monthly announcement service from Heriot-Watt University's library service which lists several dozen new sites with brief comments. Recently celebrating its 50th issue, this service aims to raise awareness of new sources of information on the Internet. Each issue attracts a readership of one or two thousand (according to their visible counter).

BUBL Information Service

http://www.bubl.ac.uk/
BUBL provides a subject-based interface to Internet resources. Submission is simple: send a message to bubl@bubl.ac.uk and include both the URL of the resource or service and a short description of its purpose and contents. The site will be visited, evaluated and catalogued before acceptance. There were over 6 million accesses to the service in the year to July 1998, some 67,000 to the Link search page. This service was originally specifically provided by and for information professionals, but has

widened its scope to the UK higher education academic and research community.

Each sector has its own directories, newsletters and gateways – the strength of a Web site, and by implication its management, is the extent to which it reflects, demonstrates and exploits the specialist knowledge that its users expect to find in its content. Part of the planning process for establishing links and entries in directories is the identification of suitable locations where your Web site address will bring visitors.

8. Direct Advertising

You may – just possibly – be in the fortunate position of having an advertising budget with which to promote your Web site. In this case there are a range of options open to you. You could simply buy advertising space in the general, professional and trade media, both printed and electronic. For example, a quarter-page advert in *Inform*, the newsletter of the Institute of Information Scientists, will cost you £115 + VAT, putting your details in front of 2,500 information professionals and experts. An electronic newsletter such as *FreePint* charges from £250 for a single insertion of a few lines in their monthly newsletter to 13,000 subscribers.

Banner Adverts

Banner advertisements can be seen everywhere on the Web. Some are hugely expensive – the corporate advertisements on the major search services, for example. Many others are free, delivered as part of schemes that links thousands of Web sites through banner exchanges. You can create a banner advertisement and pay for another site to host it, thus directing visitors your way. Careful consideration as to cost and effectiveness is needed, but if a relevant site can be identified, it can bring interested and informed visitors your way (as opposed to general sightseers).

Groups such as HyperBanner (www.hyperbanner.com) or LinkExchange (www.linkexchange.com) enable your adverts to be displayed at no cost, in exchange for showing another company's banner advert on your site. However, the fact that the banners delivered to be displayed on your site are out of your control means that this may be unlikely to appeal. The topic may be entirely inappropriate, and you have no control over the design or colours, merely over the size displayed. The other main drawback is that most of the free schemes work on a 2-1 ratio: for each two occasions on which your pages are accessed, one display of your banner is provided. This means that you provide two opportunities for visitors to leave your site for every opportunity to visit your site.

Banner adverts do have a few problems: if you host them on your site, then you are giving visitors an opportunity to leave; persuading another site to host your advert may raise the same objection. Charges on commercial sites may be anything from £10-£70 per thousand impressions, that is the times a banner is displayed. Alternatively, some sites charge on a clickthrough basis – you are charged each time a visitor actually clicks on the banner to follow the link to your site: the fee for this may be somewhere in the region of 1p-4p per click, but charged on a guaranteed minimum of several thousand – your advert remains on the site until this target is reached. In this case you are at least paying for results, but unless you actually selling products or services directly from the site, it may be hard to justify this sort of expenditure.

The most cost-effective use of a banner advert is to treat it as an illustrated reciprocal link: design the banner to be as effective as possible, then reach an agreement with a related site to exchange banners. This might just be on a related links page, or possibly on a 'higher' page, raising the profile.

Having said all that, banner adverts are notoriously ineffective (unless you are an advertising salesman). Clickthrough rates range from 3-4% for the most effective and interactive banners, down to 0.2% for static banners. This compares unfavourably with most other marketing activities such as mailshots or media advertising. Those adverts that do work have animation, primary colours and explicit exhortations to 'click here' or similar. They promote services or products directly relevant to the site on which they are hosted, so that the audience is already interested in the offer – whatever it may be.

Retain and Build

It is widely understood in marketing that it costs many times more (in money or just sheer effort) to acquire new customers then to retain existing ones. Web sites are no exception to this. Information seekers look for reliable resources that they can trust and return to on a regular basis. Whilst many people will at least check out a new resource, there has to be a good reason to bookmark that resource and use it as a regular source of information.

The range of strategies in this book apply both to the 'first look' visitor and to the regular. Ideas which add value to your site ensure that once attracted, the user stays hooked on your resource. This benefits you in two ways – firstly, a satisfied customer is a repeat visitor, who may then progress to purchasing premium (i.e. priced) services; secondly,

you increase the word-of-mouth effect, where un-
biased users recommend your site to colleagues,
discussion lists and newsgroups. Free promotion is
all the more effective for its obvious neutrality.

9. Monitoring and Measurement

Monitoring, measurement and evaluation are an essential part of any marketing activity. For the manager of a Web site, they are essential if the site is to develop and improve. Statistical measurement of Web site activity can be done in a number of ways, with varying technical requirements. When choosing which method to use, consider what information you are actually after, and to what use it will be put.

Actual numbers have only limited value in Internet planning. The difficulties in accurate measurement mean that any quoted figures are as much estimate as measurement, and many quoted surveys may use self-selected samples (i.e. by filling in forms on a Web page) which excludes those without Internet access, giving a highly skewed result.

The trends that are visible are useful, however. Even the trends provided by statistically limited online research surveys can demonstrate the growth in the potential online market, although decisions based on these figures should be treated with some caution.

Measuring Site Activity

Measurement Tools

When Web sites require investment of time and money, measurable results are required, both by management and the creative team. Measuring the effectiveness of the Web site starts with recording the raw statistics of visits. This can be done in a number of ways, as shown here. The examples provided are each just one of many potential providers of site statistics.

If you simply wish to measure site visits – the equivalent of the library gate reading – then a simple page counter may suffice, although it may be of limited accuracy, and may generate a poor impression if your site's low performance is visible to all and sundry. On the other hand of you need fuller information, in order to refocus your marketing strategy, or adapt your Web site design, then more detailed information is required.

Public Counters

A simple counter can be inserted on a page, providing a visible count of visits. Not entirely reliable or accurate, the counter merely provides a general reassurance that visits are occurring.

Pros

> Cheap (usually free).
>
> Simple – cut and paste code provided.
>
> Quick to install (or delete).
>
> Increasingly complex statistics available.

Cons

> Only as reliable as the remote site.
>
> Onscreen counters may look amateurish.
>
> Only a single page's statistics provided.
>
> Usually visible to all site visitors.
>
> Visitors who turn off images not counted.

Private Counters or Server Logs

Every Web server generates log files, which can be analysed with the appropriate software, identifying the number of visits to a page, the domain from which the visits originate, and the length of time spent at the site. WebTrends provides real-time logs importing, analysis and reporting for any Web site.

Pros

> Already part of the server software.
>
> Comprehensive statistics provided.
>
> Entirely within your site's control.

Cons

> Raw statistics may need interpretation.
>
> Some programming (or software) needed both to access & make sense of statistics.
>
> Only a single page's statistics provided.

External Site Audit

Organisations such as Audit Bureau of Circulations (www.abc.org.uk) and Nielsen Media (www.nielsen media.com) provide a full and formal auditing service in the same way they provide them for Television or Newspaper organisations.

Pros

Industry approved and recognised.

Accurate, reliable and comprehensive.

Appropriate for large, busy corporate and commercial sites whose revenue is defined by provable circulation.

Cons

Expensive and complex.

Measuring Searchability

Using your set of keywords, try and find your site through the search services. Record your ranking in the main search services, and attempt to improve your position by adding or changing keywords and re-submitting your URL. If you cannot find your site within the top 50 results, then score it as a 'not found'. Some searchers may persevere and look through hundreds of results, but more users will only go down four or five pages of ten results before trying again, or trying elsewhere. A simple spreadsheet can help keep track of how effective your efforts have been.

Rank This! is an online service that will check your ranking on the main search services. In the example below, Engineering Information (cpxweb.ei.org) ranks very highly when using the search term Compendex. This is hardly surprising of course, but nevertheless it is reassuring to the producers of the database that their own site comes out as one of the top results. A less well-designed site might come in the results below hundreds of pages of university helpsheets or database listings – still useful, but not ideal.

Searched Keyphrase: compendex
Ranked URL: http://cpxweb.ei.org
Listing Status: Found
Ranking: 2

See the AltaVista Search for 'compendex': (1)

Top 10 Listings

1) BIDS Ei Compendex/Ei Page One Service
2) Ei Compendex*Web(Ultra)
3) Ei Compendex*Plus
4) Ei Compendex Web
5) CHEST Ei Inc Agreement for Compendex
6) Ei Compendex*Web Trial Request
7) Ei Catalog -- Compendex
8) CHEST Ei-Compendex: Special Conditions

http://www.rankthis.com/

You can use the RankThis service to find keywords and design hints – conduct a search using RankThis, then compare the sites that are returned as the top ten. What keywords have they used? Have they designed the page content effectively, or simply been lucky? Learn from their success and in a few weeks (and a few URL submissions) your site should start to show up nearer to the top of the listing.

Another service that lists your position in several search services simultaneously is Position Agent (www.positionagent.com). Carrying out a search for Compendex brings the results shown in the next two illustrations. The first uses the URL for the Engineering Information home page (www.ei.org), the second uses the URL for the specific Compendex page (cpxweb.ei.org). The results differ markedly as the indexing of the different pages will show Compendex in a different level of importance.

This does not mean that the first search represents 'bad' design. Engineering Information would probably want a specific search for a particular database to go direct to the relevant page. Their well-designed site does after all have links back to their home page from all the pages within their site. Also, they could not hope to prioritise the complete range of services in the keywords used on their home page – they provide many services, and the home page is designed to be clear and concise.

Position Agent only searches through the first three pages of results – this may or may not reflect what the casual or determined searcher may do.

Evaluating Statistics

Getting visitors to come to your site once is the first step. Getting them to come back again and again, to use your site as their first stop rather than a last resort, can be a little harder. One way to ensure that your visitors return is to add so much value to their visit that they come back despite themselves. Because they have to. Because their life is incomplete without a return visit.

The measurement of the visits and the analysis of their meaning is more art than science, even in the technological environment of the Internet. Measuring visits is a start certainly. Measuring 'searchability' provides some reassurance that if they want to find you, they will be able to. But to enhance the continuous development that is the hallmark of the good Web site, a deeper understanding of the visitor's experience is required. Building in a route for feedback – with

Name	Status	Position			Page	
Alta-Vista	done		2			1
Magellan	done		1			1
Yahoo	done	–	–	–	–	–
Excite	done		2			1
HotBot	done		1			1
WebCrawler	done		1			1
InfoSeek	done		1			1
Lycos	done	–	–	–	–	–
LinkStar	done		1			1
Galaxy	done	–	–	–	–	–

Compendex and www.ei.org

Name	Status	Position			Page	
Alta-Vista	done		7			1
Magellan	done	–	–	–	–	–
Yahoo	done	–	–	–	–	–
Excite	done		8			1
HotBot	done	–	–	–	–	–
WebCrawler	done	–	–	–	–	–
InfoSeek	done	1	5			2
Lycos	done	–	–	–	–	–
LinkStar	done	–	–	–	–	–
Galaxy	done	–	–	–	–	–

Compendex and cpxweb.ei.org

email comment forms, customer satisfaction surveys and full server statistics are all useful sources of information. Evaluating this information is the next step – can you rely on its accuracy? Can you understand the information provided? Can you decide what action to take next?

Whether this evaluation is a solitary activity, or a good reason for another committee, will of course depend on the nature of your Web site. Whichever is chosen, a firm understanding of the activities taken and needed to promote a Web site will inform and explain the data received from any evaluative exercise.

From the evaluative exercise comes the next stage of the promotional strategy – starting the cycle all over again. Monitor, evaluate, improve.

Appendix: Web Site Marketing and Promotion Newsletters

Market Position Newsletter

To join send an email to subscribe@webposition.com

To leave send an email to unsubscribe@webposition.com

or register at http://www.marketposition.com/

Fletcher Research Internet Analysis newsletter

To join send an email to subscribe@fletch.co.uk with the word subscribe in the subject line

To leave subscribe@fletch.co.uk with the word desubscribe in the subject line

or register at http://www.fletch.co.uk/

Free Pint

To subscribe or unsubscribe, visit the Web site at http://www.freepint.co.uk/

Web Site Journal

To join send an email to feedback@websitejournal.com with the word subscribe in the subject line

To leave follow instructions sent to you on subscribing.

Glossary

Crawler (or Robot, or Spider)
Software that automatically follows links on Web pages, downloading each page as it goes, for indexing onto a database.

Database
The collection of information against which queries are run: the Internet is one large database.

Directory
In this context a structured database, searched by following links through levels and sub-levels of categories. Categorisation and classification done by humans, sometimes even librarians(!).

Engine
Technically, the software used to search through a dataset or database (e.g. HotBot uses the Inktomi search engine).

Filtering
Reducing the hits - or the level of information in general - by matching searches by comparing the database against a profile or selection of keywords.

Index
In this context a database that has been structured for efficient data retrieval, with searches typically based on keywords. Normally human-free.

Keyword
Term used to score the search results and place them in order of relevance.

META tags
HTML code use to provide information about the Web page or its creator. Does not appear on the screen, but may be used to affect the indexing of a document.

Robot
See Crawler.

Service
Any Web site providing a search facility.

Spider
See Crawler.

Tool
An individual function within a service.

Note
In practice, the terms database, search service, search tool and search engine are used interchangeably.

Aslib Know How Guides